Weekly Planner

Monday

Tuesday

Wednesday

Thursday

Friday

Saturday

Sunday

Notes

Weekly Planner

Monday

Tuesday

Wednesday

Thursday

Friday

Saturday

Sunday

Notes

Weekly Planner

Monday

Tuesday

Wednesday

Thursday

Friday

Saturday

Sunday

Notes

Weekly Planner

Monday

Tuesday

Wednesday

Thursday

Friday

Saturday

Sunday

to-do

Notes

Weekly Planner

Monday

Tuesday

Wednesday

Thursday

Friday

Saturday

Sunday

to-do

Notes

Weekly Planner

Monday

Tuesday

Wednesday

Thursday

Friday

Saturday

Sunday

To-do

Notes

Weekly Planner

Monday

Tuesday

Wednesday

Thursday

Friday

Saturday

Sunday

to-do

Notes

Weekly Planner

Monday

Tuesday

Wednesday

Thursday

Friday

Saturday

Sunday

to-do

Notes

Weekly Planner

Monday

Tuesday

Wednesday

Thursday

Friday

Saturday

Sunday

To-do

-
-
-
-
-
-
-
-
-
-
-
-
-

Notes

Weekly Planner

Monday

Tuesday

Wednesday

Thursday

Friday

Saturday

Sunday

to-do

Notes

Weekly Planner

Monday

Tuesday

Wednesday

Thursday

Friday

Saturday

Sunday

Notes

Weekly Planner

Monday

Tuesday

Wednesday

Thursday

Friday

Saturday

Sunday

to-do

-
-
-
-
-
-
-
-
-
-
-
-

Notes

Weekly Planner

Monday

Tuesday

Wednesday

Thursday

Friday

Saturday

Sunday

To-do

Notes

Weekly Planner

Monday

Tuesday

Wednesday

Thursday

Friday

Saturday

Sunday

To-do

Notes

Weekly Planner

Monday

Tuesday

Wednesday

Thursday

Friday

Saturday

Sunday

To-do

Notes

Weekly Planner

Monday

Tuesday

Wednesday

Thursday

Friday

Saturday

Sunday

to-do

Notes

Weekly Planner

Monday

Tuesday

Wednesday

Thursday

Friday

Saturday

Sunday

To-do

Notes

Weekly Planner

Monday

Tuesday

Wednesday

Thursday

Friday

Saturday

Sunday

Notes

Weekly Planner

Monday

Tuesday

Wednesday

Thursday

Friday

Saturday

Sunday

To-do

Notes

Weekly Planner

Monday

Tuesday

Wednesday

Thursday

Friday

Saturday

Sunday

to-do

Notes

Weekly Planner

Monday

Tuesday

Wednesday

Thursday

Friday

Saturday

Sunday

to-do

-
-
-
-
-
-
-
-
-
-
-
-
-

Notes

Weekly Planner

Monday

Tuesday

Wednesday

Thursday

Friday

Saturday

Sunday

to-do

Notes

Weekly Planner

Monday

Tuesday

Wednesday

Thursday

Friday

Saturday

Sunday

to-do

Notes

Weekly Planner

Monday

Tuesday

Wednesday

Thursday

Friday

Saturday

Sunday

to-do

- _____
- _____
- _____
- _____
- _____
- _____
- _____
- _____
- _____
- _____
- _____
- _____

Notes

Weekly Planner

Monday

Tuesday

Wednesday

Thursday

Friday

Saturday

Sunday

to-do

Notes

Weekly Planner

Monday

Tuesday

Wednesday

Thursday

Friday

Saturday

Sunday

to-do

Notes

Weekly Planner

Monday

Tuesday

Wednesday

Thursday

Friday

Saturday

Sunday

to-do

Notes

Weekly Planner

Monday

Tuesday

Wednesday

Thursday

Friday

Saturday

Sunday

to-do

Notes

Weekly Planner

Monday

Tuesday

Wednesday

Thursday

Friday

Saturday

Sunday

To-do

Notes

Weekly Planner

Monday

Tuesday

Wednesday

Thursday

Friday

Saturday

Sunday

To-do

Notes

Weekly Planner

Monday

Tuesday

Wednesday

Thursday

Friday

Saturday

Sunday

to-do

Notes

Weekly Planner

Monday

Tuesday

Wednesday

Thursday

Friday

Saturday

Sunday

to-do

Notes

Weekly Planner

Monday

Tuesday

Wednesday

Thursday

Friday

Saturday

Sunday

to-do

Notes

Weekly Planner

Monday

Tuesday

Wednesday

Thursday

Friday

Saturday

Sunday

to-do

-
-
-
-
-
-
-
-
-
-
-
-

Notes

Weekly Planner

Monday

Tuesday

Wednesday

Thursday

Friday

Saturday

Sunday

to-do

Notes

Weekly Planner

Monday

Tuesday

Wednesday

Thursday

Friday

Saturday

Sunday

To-do

Notes

Weekly Planner

Monday

Tuesday

Wednesday

Thursday

Friday

Saturday

Sunday

to-do

Notes

Weekly Planner

Monday

Tuesday

Wednesday

Thursday

Friday

Saturday

Sunday

Notes

Weekly Planner

Monday

Tuesday

Wednesday

Thursday

Friday

Saturday

Sunday

To-do

Notes

Weekly Planner

Monday

Tuesday

Wednesday

Thursday

Friday

Saturday

Sunday

to-do

Notes

Weekly Planner

Monday

Tuesday

Wednesday

Thursday

Friday

Saturday

Sunday

to-do

-
-
-
-
-
-
-
-
-
-
-
-
-

Notes

Weekly Planner

Monday

Tuesday

Wednesday

Thursday

Friday

Saturday

Sunday

to-do

Notes

Weekly Planner

Monday

Tuesday

Wednesday

Thursday

Friday

Saturday

Sunday

to-do

Notes

Weekly Planner

Monday

Tuesday

Wednesday

Thursday

Friday

Saturday

Sunday

to-do

Notes

Weekly Planner

Monday

Tuesday

Wednesday

Thursday

Friday

Saturday

Sunday

To-do

Notes

Weekly Planner

Monday

Tuesday

Wednesday

Thursday

Friday

Saturday

Sunday

to-do

Notes

Weekly Planner

Monday

Tuesday

Wednesday

Thursday

Friday

Saturday

Sunday

To-do

Notes

Weekly Planner

Monday

Tuesday

Wednesday

Thursday

Friday

Saturday

Sunday

Notes

Weekly Planner

Monday

Tuesday

Wednesday

Thursday

Friday

Saturday

Sunday

To-do

Notes

Weekly Planner

Monday

Tuesday

Wednesday

Thursday

Friday

Saturday

Sunday

to-do

Notes

Weekly Planner

Monday

Tuesday

Wednesday

Thursday

Friday

Saturday

Sunday

To-do

-
-
-
-
-
-
-
-
-
-
-
-
-
-

Notes

Weekly Planner

Monday

Tuesday

Wednesday

Thursday

Friday

Saturday

Sunday

To-do

Notes

Weekly Planner

Monday

Tuesday

Wednesday

Thursday

Friday

Saturday

Sunday

to-do

Notes

Weekly Planner

Monday

Tuesday

Wednesday

Thursday

Friday

Saturday

Sunday

to-do

Notes

Weekly Planner

Monday

Tuesday

Wednesday

Thursday

Friday

Saturday

Sunday

to-do

Notes

Weekly Planner

Monday

Tuesday

Wednesday

Thursday

Friday

Saturday

Sunday

to-do

Notes

Weekly Planner

Monday

Tuesday

Wednesday

Thursday

Friday

Saturday

Sunday

to-do

Notes

Weekly Planner

Monday

Tuesday

Wednesday

Thursday

Friday

Saturday

Sunday

to-do

Notes

Weekly Planner

Monday

Tuesday

Wednesday

Thursday

Friday

Saturday

Sunday

to-do

Notes

Weekly Planner

Monday

Tuesday

Wednesday

Thursday

Friday

Saturday

Sunday

to-do

-
-
-
-
-
-
-
-
-
-
-
-
-

Notes

Weekly Planner

Monday

Tuesday

Wednesday

Thursday

Friday

Saturday

Sunday

Notes

Weekly Planner

Monday

Tuesday

Wednesday

Thursday

Friday

Saturday

Sunday

to-do

Notes

Weekly Planner

Monday

Tuesday

Wednesday

Thursday

Friday

Saturday

Sunday

Notes

Weekly Planner

Monday

Tuesday

Wednesday

Thursday

Friday

Saturday

Sunday

to-do

Notes

Weekly Planner

Monday

Tuesday

Wednesday

Thursday

Friday

Saturday

Sunday

to-do

Notes

Weekly Planner

Monday

Tuesday

Wednesday

Thursday

Friday

Saturday

Sunday

to-do

Notes

Weekly Planner

Monday

Tuesday

Wednesday

Thursday

Friday

Saturday

Sunday

To-do

Notes

Weekly Planner

Monday

Tuesday

Wednesday

Thursday

Friday

Saturday

Sunday

to-do

Notes

Weekly Planner

Monday

Tuesday

Wednesday

Thursday

Friday

Saturday

Sunday

To-do

Notes

Weekly Planner

Monday

Tuesday

Wednesday

Thursday

Friday

Saturday

Sunday

To-do

Notes

Weekly Planner

Monday

Tuesday

Wednesday

Thursday

Friday

Saturday

Sunday

to-do

Notes

Weekly Planner

Monday

Tuesday

Wednesday

Thursday

Friday

Saturday

Sunday

to-do

Notes

Weekly Planner

Monday

Tuesday

Wednesday

Thursday

Friday

Saturday

Sunday

to-do

-
-
-
-
-
-
-
-
-
-
-
-
-

Notes

Weekly Planner

Monday

Tuesday

Wednesday

Thursday

Friday

Saturday

Sunday

to-do

Notes

Weekly Planner

Monday

Tuesday

Wednesday

Thursday

Friday

Saturday

Sunday

to-do

Notes

Weekly Planner

Monday

Tuesday

Wednesday

Thursday

Friday

Saturday

Sunday

To-do

Notes

Weekly Planner

Monday

Tuesday

Wednesday

Thursday

Friday

Saturday

Sunday

To-do

-
-
-
-
-
-
-
-
-
-
-
-

Notes

Weekly Planner

Monday

Tuesday

Wednesday

Thursday

Friday

Saturday

Sunday

to-do

Notes

Weekly Planner

Monday

Tuesday

Wednesday

Thursday

Friday

Saturday

Sunday

to-do

Notes

Weekly Planner

Monday

Tuesday

Wednesday

Thursday

Friday

Saturday

Sunday

to-do

Notes

Weekly Planner

Monday

Tuesday

Wednesday

Thursday

Friday

Saturday

Sunday

to-do

-
-
-
-
-
-
-
-
-
-
-
-
-
-

Notes

Weekly Planner

Monday

Tuesday

Wednesday

Thursday

Friday

Saturday

Sunday

to-do

Notes

Weekly Planner

Monday

Tuesday

Wednesday

Thursday

Friday

Saturday

Sunday

to-do

Notes

Weekly Planner

Monday

Tuesday

Wednesday

Thursday

Friday

Saturday

Sunday

to-do

Notes

Weekly Planner

Monday

Tuesday

Wednesday

Thursday

Friday

Saturday

Sunday

to-do

-
-
-
-
-
-
-
-
-
-
-
-

Notes

Weekly Planner

Monday

Tuesday

Wednesday

Thursday

Friday

Saturday

Sunday

to-do

Notes

Weekly Planner

Monday

Tuesday

Wednesday

Thursday

Friday

Saturday

Sunday

To-do

Notes

Weekly Planner

Monday

Tuesday

Wednesday

Thursday

Friday

Saturday

Sunday

to-do

Notes

Weekly Planner

Monday

Tuesday

Wednesday

Thursday

Friday

Saturday

Sunday

to-do

Notes

Weekly Planner

Monday

Tuesday

Wednesday

Thursday

Friday

Saturday

Sunday

To-do

Notes

Weekly Planner

Monday

Tuesday

Wednesday

Thursday

Friday

Saturday

Sunday

To-do

Notes

Weekly Planner

Monday

Tuesday

Wednesday

Thursday

Friday

Saturday

Sunday

Notes

Weekly Planner

Monday

Tuesday

Wednesday

Thursday

Friday

Saturday

Sunday

to-do

Notes

Weekly Planner

Monday

Tuesday

Wednesday

Thursday

Friday

Saturday

Sunday

to-do

Notes

Weekly Planner

Monday

Tuesday

Wednesday

Thursday

Friday

Saturday

Sunday

To-do

Notes

Weekly Planner

Monday

Tuesday

Wednesday

Thursday

Friday

Saturday

Sunday

Notes

Weekly Planner

Monday

Tuesday

Wednesday

Thursday

Friday

Saturday

Sunday

to-do

Notes

Weekly Planner

Monday

Tuesday

Wednesday

Thursday

Friday

Saturday

Sunday

Notes

Weekly Planner

Monday

Tuesday

Wednesday

Thursday

Friday

Saturday

Sunday

Notes

Weekly Planner

Monday

Tuesday

Wednesday

Thursday

Friday

Saturday

Sunday

to-do

-
-
-
-
-
-
-
-
-
-
-
-

Notes

Weekly Planner

Monday

Tuesday

Wednesday

Thursday

Friday

Saturday

Sunday

to-do

Notes

Weekly Planner

Monday

Tuesday

Wednesday

Thursday

Friday

Saturday

Sunday

to-do

Notes

Weekly Planner

Monday

Tuesday

Wednesday

Thursday

Friday

Saturday

Sunday

To-do

Notes

Weekly Planner

Monday

Tuesday

Wednesday

Thursday

Friday

Saturday

Sunday

to-do

Notes

Weekly Planner

Monday

Tuesday

Wednesday

Thursday

Friday

Saturday

Sunday

to-do

Notes

Weekly Planner

Monday

Tuesday

Wednesday

Thursday

Friday

Saturday

Sunday

to-do

Notes

Weekly Planner

Monday

Tuesday

Wednesday

Thursday

Friday

Saturday

Sunday

To-do

Notes

Weekly Planner

Monday

Tuesday

Wednesday

Thursday

Friday

Saturday

Sunday

To-do

-
-
-
-
-
-
-
-
-
-
-
-
-

Notes

Weekly Planner

Monday

Tuesday

Wednesday

Thursday

Friday

Saturday

Sunday

To-do

Notes

Weekly Planner

Monday

Tuesday

Wednesday

Thursday

Friday

Saturday

Sunday

to-do

Notes

Printed in Great Britain
by Amazon

33799506R00066